God's
Bible Pathway
For Children

Written by

Jane Spring
Queensland, Australia

Edited & Illustrated by

Don & Bonnie Burrows

Edited & Formatted by

John & Hiedi Vogele

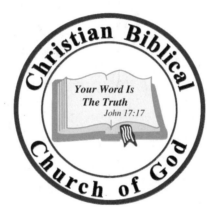

ISBN: 978-0-9819787-1-0
©2009
Christian Biblical Church of God
Post Office Box 1442
Hollister, California 95024-1442

Manufactured by Thomson-Shore, Dexter, MI (USA); RMA563TB335, October, 2009

My name is:

_____

I am _____ years old.

I want to learn.

Teach me God's pathway.

Please read to me.

Table of Contents

Preface iv

God's Bible Pathway for Children v

Do Not Enter into the Path of the Wicked . vii

In the Beginning Was God 1

God Made the Angels and the Earth 4

Lucifer's Rebellion 5

Start of the Seven Days of Creation 9

Garden of Eden 16

God Shows Adam and Eve Two Trees . . . 17

Adam and Eve Disobey God 19

God Tells Noah to Build an Ark 22

Noah Comes Out of the Ark 27

Nimrod Starts Religion and Rebellion . . . 29

Tower of Babel 30

God calls Abram 34

Israel Goes into Egypt 40

God Calls Moses 42

Out of Egypt and into the Wilderness . . . 46

God Spoke the Ten Commandments 49

Out of the Wilderness and
        into the Promised Land 54

Samuel as a Child 55

Israel Wants a King 57

King David 58

Daniel in the Lions' Den 64

Birth of Jesus 70

Life of Jesus 72

Death of Jesus 74
Resurrection of Jesus 76
Satan Locked Up 82
Jesus Christ Rules the World 84
Great White Throne Judgment 88
God's Pathway 92
The World's Way 93
Analyzing Peoples' False Ideas About God . 94
God's Special Commandment for Children . . 99
How to Pray 102
Special Way to Study the
        Book of Proverbs 103
The Ten Commandments 104
What Should I Pray About and Who
        Should I Pray To? 105

Preface

This book is written for children to help them understand how the world was made and the purpose for their life. Originally, I only made bare sketches drawn as simple and brief as possible so a child can understand. The Christian Biblical Church of God graciously asked my permission to make this presentation into a full scale book. Don Burrows reformatted the text I wrote and Bonnie Burrows drew the illustrations. I gratefully thank them for doing so. Parents and grandparents are encouraged to read to their children and grandchildren.

Author — *Jane Spring*
Queensland, Australia

God's Bible Pathway For Children

The Pathway of Life
Bible Verses to Memorize

Jesus said, "I am the way, and the truth
and the life..." John 14:6

In the way of righteousness *is* life, and in that
pathway *there is* no death. Proverbs 12:28

You will make known to Me the path of life;
in Your presence is fullness of joy.
Psalms 16:11

My steps have held fast to your paths,
my feet have not slipped.
Psalms 17:5

He leads me in the paths of righteousness
for His name's sake. Psalms 23:3

Show me Your ways, O LORD; teach me
Your paths. Lead me in Your truth and
teach me... Psalms 25:4-5

Even a child is known by his own doings,
whether his work is pure and
whether *it is* right. Proverbs 20:11

All the paths of the LORD are mercy and truth,
Psalms 25:10

Make me to walk in the path of Your commandments, for I delight in them. Psalms 119:35

Your word is a lamp to my feet and a light
to my path. Psalms 119:105

...take hold of the paths of life—in order that
you may walk in the way of good and keep the
paths of the righteous. Proverbs 2:19-20

Trust in the LORD with all your heart, and
lean not to your own understanding. In all your
ways acknowledge Him, and He shall
direct your paths. Proverbs 3:5-6

Hear, O my son, and receive my sayings; and the
years of your life *shall be* many. Proverbs 4:10

The path of the just *is* as the shining light, that
shines more and more to the perfect day.
Proverbs 4:18

Do Not Enter into the Path of the Wicked

Let your eyes look right on, and let your eyelids look straight before you. Ponder the path of your feet, and all your ways *will be* established.
Do not turn to the right hand nor to the left; remove your foot from evil. Proverbs 4:25-27

My son, if sinners entice you, do not consent...
Proverbs 1:10

My son, do not walk in the way with them! Keep back your foot from their path, for their feet run to evil and make haste to shed blood. Proverbs 1:15-16

Enter not into the path of the wicked, and go not into the way of evil *men*. Avoid it; do not go in it; turn from it, and pass on! Proverbs 4:14-15

The way of the wicked *is* as darkness; they know not at what they stumble. Proverbs 4:19

There is a way which seems right to a man, but the end thereof *is* the way of death...
The backslider in heart shall be filled with his own ways, but a good man *shall be satisfied* with his own actions.
The simple believes every word, but the wise *man* watches his step. A wise one fears and departs from evil, but the fool rages and is confident.
Proverbs 14:12-16

How the
World
Began
and
Beyond

In the Beginning Was God

Everyone needs to know how and why the world started, so a book was written. The book tells us how to live and why we were made. God inspired some people to write what He wanted all people to know. It is a very big book and is sometimes hard to understand, but it tells us the way that is the truth. Today, very few people believe and love God. Neither do they read God's book. So they do not know the gateway that leads to life.

The book we have to read is called the Holy Bible. When we read the Bible, we find the truth. For God is true and His Word is true.

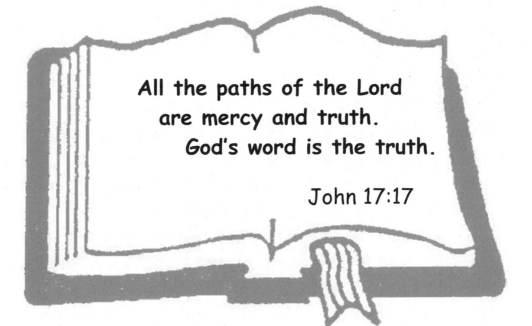

All the paths of the Lord
are mercy and truth.
God's word is the truth.

John 17:17

There have always been two almighty, all-powerful beings who are God. They know everything and understand everything. These two great God-beings have the same shape as people. They have arms, hands, legs, feet, a body and a face, but they are much, Much, MUCH greater than people, because They are spirit. They are not flesh like people who will die.

They have no beginning because They have always existed. They have no end because They cannot die, except for the One of the God family Who chose to come to earth as a man and our Savior to die for the sins of the people that He had created.

These great beings are called God the Father and God the Son. They are spirit, which our eyes cannot see, kind of like the wind or electricity.

God the Father and God the Son live in heaven above the earth. Our minds cannot understand how much God the Father and God the Son know or how mighty they are. A man named John had a vision. A vision is a picture in the air, in the mind or in the sky instead of on paper. In the vision John saw that God the Son had hair white like wool, as white as snow and God the Son's eyes were as a flame of fire. His feet were like brass, as if they burned in a fire. God the Son's voice sounds like a huge waterfall and a great trumpet.

John said he saw a throne in heaven and God sitting on it, Who looked like a jasper stone and a sardine stone in His glory. And around the throne was a rainbow like an emerald.

Around the throne are twenty-four smaller thrones with twenty-four elders sitting on them. Out from God's throne came lightning, thundering and voices.

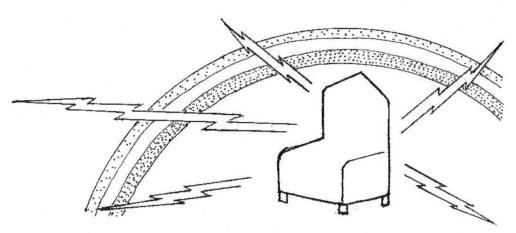

The third Heaven is where God's throne is.
God says, "The heaven is My throne and the earth is My footstool."

The second heaven is the sun, moon and stars.

The first heaven is the air and clouds around the earth.

God Made the Angels and the Earth

God made three very strong angels—Michael the archangel, Gabriel and Lucifer. But Lucifer rebelled, so God changed his name to Satan, the ancient serpent. God also made many other angels that are not as powerful. God made angels of spirit so they can't die and they can also appear as men.

God made the universe, the earth, the oceans, fish and whales and many other creatures. He created the trees, plants, flowers and grass.

Lucifer's Rebellion

Then God commanded Lucifer and the angels to look after the earth, tending trees, plants and dinosaurs, as other animals and creeping creatures and the whole earth.

After a while Lucifer became greedy, selfish, jealous and vain. Lucifer said, "I will be like the Most High God." Lucifer went up to heaven to fight God. Michael and his angels had a huge war against Satan and his angels.

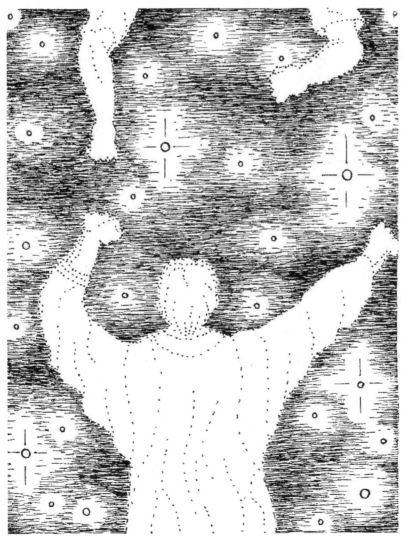

And there was war in heaven; Michael and his angels warred against the dragon, and the dragon and his angels fought. But they did not win. They lost and their place was not around any more in heaven. And the great dragon was cast out, the ancient serpent who is called the Devil and Satan, who is deceiving the whole world; he was cast down to the earth, and his angels were cast down with him.

Jesus said that He saw Satan fall as lightning from heaven.

Lucifer and his angels were thrown down from heaven like lightning and fell to the earth. In this gigantic fight, it seems many big stars, planets, asteroids and comets in the universe were thrown around. Some big pieces hit the earth so hard all the animals died and were buried under tons of dirt and rock and they became fossils under the earth. Everything was covered with ash, dust, smoke and water. The light of the sun, moon and stars was blocked out. The whole earth became dark and cold, no light or heat—and everything died.

A long, long time passed. The entire earth was covered with water and it was very dark, cold, and empty—nothing was alive.

The Bible tells us, "And the earth was without form and empty; and darkness was upon the face of the deep" (Genesis 1:2).

Start of the Seven Days of Creation

After a very long time God came down and, with His great power, cleared away the waters that covered the earth, and made light. The light was day and the dark was night. God measures a day from sunset to sunset, so the evening and the morning were the first day.

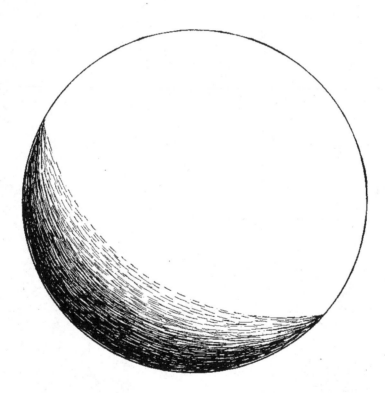

On the second day God made the air and clouds, which is the sky. The evening and the morning were the second day.

On the third day God made the water to gather in the sea and the dry land to appear. God made the earth to grow grass, herbs and fruit trees of every kind. God made all the different kinds of trees and plants. The evening and the morning were the third day.

On the fourth day God set the sun, moon, stars and the earth in their right orbits. The sun, moon, earth, and stars had to be in the correct place so there would be days, months, seasons and years. The evening and morning were the fourth day.

On the fifth day God made birds, fish, whales and all creatures that live in the sea. The evening and the morning were the fifth day.

On the sixth day God created livestock and all the other beasts of the earth and everything that creeps. God saw that it was good. God said, "Let Us make man in Our shape after the way We look. Let him rule the fish, birds, cattle, the earth and everything." God put into all living things the way for each one to make more of their kind. The evening and the morning were the sixth day.

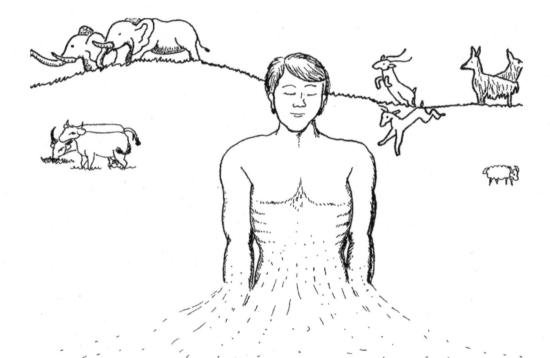

And the Lord God formed man from the dust of the ground and breathed into his nostrils the breath of life... His name was Adam. The Lord God caused a deep sleep to fall upon him and God took one of his ribs and closed up the flesh. From the rib, which God took, He made a woman and her name was Eve.

On the seventh day God rested from all His work. God blessed the seventh day and made it holy and told man to keep it holy so we will remember Who the Great Creator is. The evening and the morning were the seventh day.

The Sabbath, which is the seventh day of the week (Saturday today), was made for people to rest from work like God rested from all His work.

Garden of Eden

God planted a garden with many fruit trees and many pretty flowers. God watered it with a mist. The man named Adam and the woman named Eve were married by God. They were put in the garden to look after it. God told Adam and Eve how to live and what was right and good. The garden where they lived was called Eden.

God Shows Adam and Eve Two Trees

God had planted two trees in the middle of the Garden of Eden. One tree was called the Tree of Life and the other tree was called the Tree of the Knowledge of Good and Evil.

God told Adam and Eve they could eat the fruit from all the trees but one.

God told Adam and Eve not to eat the fruit from the Tree of the Knowledge of Good and Evil. God told Adam and Eve that if they ate the fruit from the Tree of the Knowledge of Good and Evil, that they would bring death on themselves and all people. Later, God told them that all people would have troubles, sorrows and death because of what they had done.

*Tree of the Knowledge
of Good & Evil*

Tree of Life

Satan the Devil made himself to look like a snake. Satan told the woman that if she ate fruit from the Tree of the Knowledge of Good and Evil, she would become like God. The woman listened to the devil, and ate of the tree, then gave some fruit to Adam and he ate it.

Tree of the Knowledge of Good & Evil

Adam and Eve Disobey God

Satan started all the disobedience against God and all trouble and rebellion. Satan is the power of the air moving peoples' minds. Listening to Satan has changed the nature of people and animals. People don't want to obey God. Some Animals are frightened of people and some animals eat other animals and people.

God told Adam, "Because you have listened to your wife and have eaten from the tree of which I commanded you saying; you shall not eat of it, Cursed is the ground... Thorns and also thistles shall it bring forth. In the sweat of your face shall you eat bread... for dust you are and unto dust shall you return" (Genesis 3:17-19).

God drove the man and woman out of the Garden of Eden and set cherubim (angels) with flaming swords to stop anyone going near the Tree of Life.

Adam and Eve had to go out and work extra hard to live by digging the ground to grow their food.

Adam and Eve's first two sons were Cain and Abel. After they grew up to be young men, they had troubles. Abel obeyed God by offering the correct sacrifice, but Cain made an offering to God that he devised in his own heart. God told Cain that He would not accept his evil offering and told him to repent. Cain became angry at God and did not repent. He also was jealous of Abel and killed him, so God punished Cain for his wickedness and rebellion by placing a mark on him. Then God sent him and the rest of his family to live in the land of wandering. But, Cain and his descendants continued to rebel against God, even to this day.

Adam and Eve had many more children and grandchildren as did Cain and his wicked family. It was about 1,500 years after creation, when the descendants of Cain and most of the other descendants of Adam and Eve had sinned so greatly and multiplied their wickedness, that their every thought was only evil.

"And the LORD saw that the wickedness of man was great on the earth, and every imagination of the thoughts of his heart was only evil continually. And the LORD repented that He had made man on the earth, and He was grieved in His heart. And the LORD said, 'I will destroy man whom I have created from the face of the earth, both man and beast, and the crawling thing, and the fowl of the air; for I repent that I have made them'" (Genesis 6:5-7).

God Told Noah to Build an Ark

One man named Noah obeyed God and found grace in His sight. He kept God's commandments and laws on how to live and did what was right. Because Noah had obeyed God, he was told to build a big ship, called an ark. The ark was to save him and his family from the flood, plus the animals, crawling things and birds that God would select. When the ark was finished, God caused the animals, the crawling things and birds to come into the ark by pairs.

God was sad that He had to destroy all that He had created, but their wickedness was so bad that He had to punish them for their sins. So, because of the wickedness of the people, God caused a great flood to cover the whole earth to destroy every living thing that was not in the ark, except the fish.

It took Noah a long time to make the ark because it was very big. When the ark was finished, Noah, his wife, their three sons and their wives collected a lot of food for the animals and stored it in the ark.

God made all the animals He wanted to save go into the ark.

God said, "You shall take with you every clean animal by sevens, the male and female. And take two of the animals that *are* not clean, the male and female" (Genesis 7:2).

Seven days later it started to rain. It rained for forty days and forty nights, and water burst out of the earth and out of the heavens.

The rest of the people and animals that were outside the ark drowned because the flood covered the whole earth, covering the highest mountains by fifty feet.

Noah Comes Out of the Ark

After many days the flood stopped and the mountains appeared. The ark landed near Mount Ararat. After many more days the waters were dried up from off the earth and went back into the rivers and seas.

Then, God opened the door of the ark and Noah's family and all the animals came out. God put a rainbow in the sky. God told Noah the rainbow was a sign to all people that He will never destroy the earth with a flood again.

Noah and his sons, Shem, Ham, and Japheth, and their wives, went out and started to fill the earth again with people. They had many children. Shem is the father of the white people; Ham is the father of the black people; Japheth is the father of the yellow people.

God said to Noah and his sons, "Be fruitful and multiply, and replenish the earth" (Genesis 9:1).

Nimrod Starts Religion and Rebellion

Ham and his wife had grandchildren. One of his grandsons was named Nimrod.

Nimrod grew to be a very strong man, and he did not like or obey God. Nimrod taught the people false religion. The people did evil things and again made idols of wood, stone, gold and other metals. The people began to trust in the sun, moon, and stars. The people even began to believe that the sun, moon and stars were gods and that they should worship them. Nimrod helped people forget God's ways, so the people believed his lies. They worshiped false gods and idols, and trusted them instead of the true God.

False religions of men are made with the help of Satan the devil. He causes people to disobey and to rebel against God.

When we do not obey God, we cannot understand why He has made people.

Tower of Babel

Nimrod and all the people came to a wide flat plain and they said, "Come, let us build us a city and a tower, *with* its top reaching into the heavens" (Genesis 11:4). God was angry. God said, "Behold, the people *are* one and they all have one language... and they will do anything they think they would like to do." God decided to mix up the language so the people would not understand each other.

The people could not understand each other because their speech was confused. Then they stopped building the tower. The name of the tower was Babel because the Lord God mixed up their language.

Then, God scattered the people all over the earth. But they still followed Satan and kept the religion Nimrod devised. They made evil things like idols of brass, gold, wood, and stone to worship as gods. They followed wicked ways by practicing witchcraft, wizardry and all the false and lying things God hates. He hates the evil ways because they bring trouble and in them is no hope or future.

These are some of
the idols and agents
of Satan the Devil,
who is the enemy
of God.

God Calls Abram

Shem and his wife had children. One of Shem's descendants was named Abram. Abram obeyed God. God told Abram to leave his father's house and go to another land with his wife Sarai. God changed Abram's name to Abraham and Sarai to Sarah.

Abraham had cattle, camels, horses and sheep, and lived out in the hills. He had people called servants who worked for him. Abraham obeyed God and kept His laws.

God told Abraham He would bless him and his children because Abraham obeyed God's commandments and laws on how to live in a caring, kind and loving way. Abraham became the father of many nations.

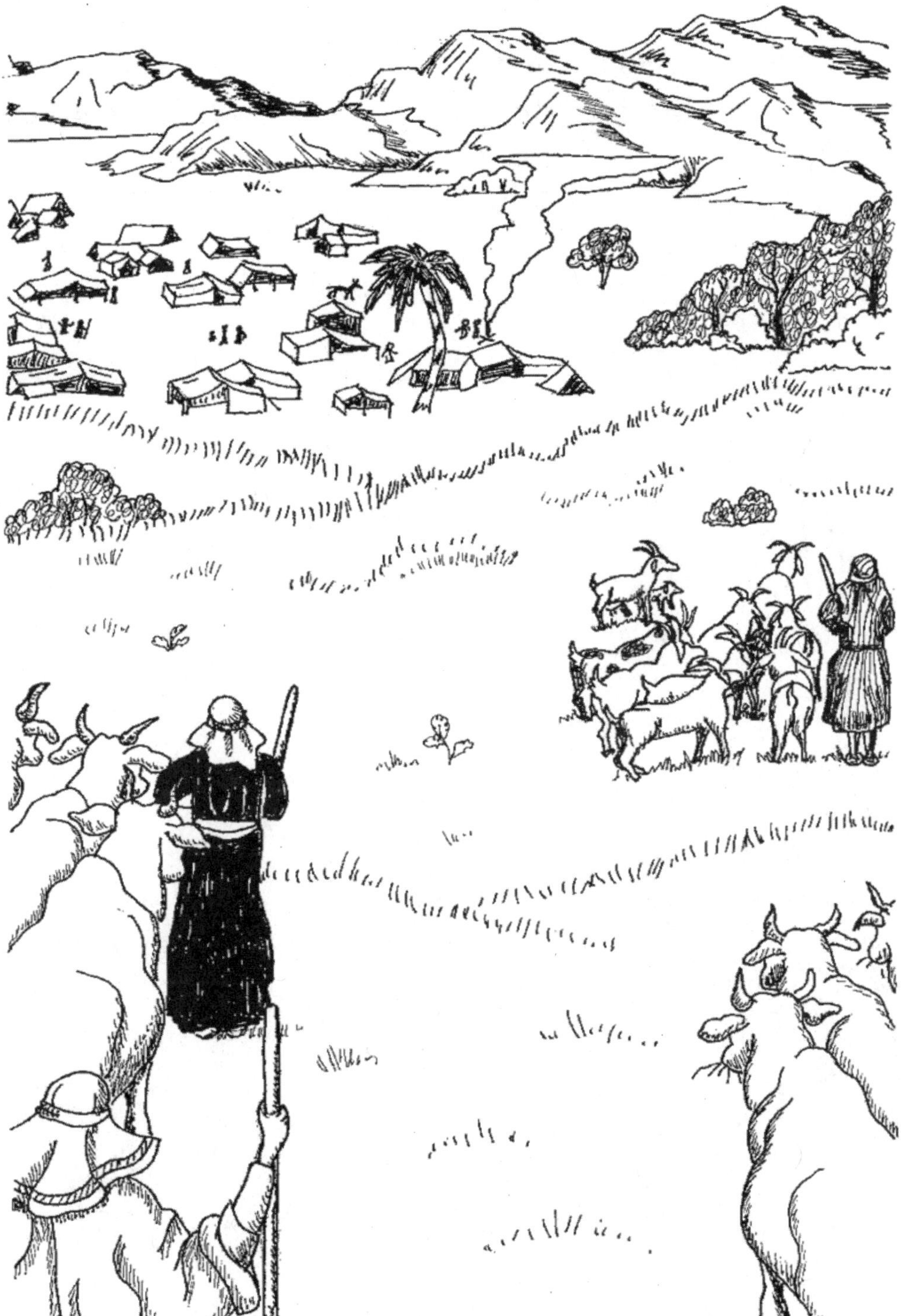

When Abraham and his wife, Sarah, were old, God made it possible for her to have a baby boy. They named him Isaac.

Isaac grew up, married, and had a son named Jacob. After Jacob married he had twelve sons. God changed Jacob's name to Israel because he learned to obey God.

One of Israel's sons, whom he loved very much, was named Joseph. He made him a "coat of many colors."

Some of Joseph's brothers hated him because he had a dream that all the brothers would kneel to him.

Because of that dream and because he was their father's favorite son, they put him in a big hole and sold him into slavery and he was taken to the country of Egypt by his masters. .

God watched over Joseph. The Egyptian King, called Pharaoh, made Joseph the second in command.

Israel Goes into Egypt

The place where Israel lived became very dry because there was no rain for years. Later, Israel and the rest of his family went to Egypt to buy grain for his cattle and sheep. Joseph recognized his brothers. He told them to bring back Benjamin. They did not know Joseph was their lost brother who they had sold into slavery because of jealousy. The brothers had taken Joseph's coat of many "colors" and put blood on it. They took it to their father, Israel, and said a lion had killed Joseph. Israel cried for Joseph. After many years, Israel found Joseph alive. There was much joy! Joseph forgave his brothers and said God wanted it to happen. They moved to Egypt and lived there for many years and had lots of children.

The children of Israel were called Israelites. The Israelites grew into a nation of many people while they lived in Egypt. When a new Pharaoh ruled Egypt, the Israelites were made slaves to the Egyptians. They forced the Israelites to work very hard.

The Egyptians did not know anything about the true God. The Egyptians thought that things like the sun, moon, stars and even snakes, fish, frogs and alligators were gods. They believed these had power to watch over them and help them in times of trouble. The Egyptians followed Satan's way, trusting in lies.

God Calls Moses

The Israelites had so many children that the Egyptian Pharaoh ordered the Israelite baby boys to be killed. One Israelite mother put her baby boy into a basket-boat in the river. The baby was found by the daughter of Pharaoh. She thought the water god had sent the baby boy to her. Pharaoh's daughter named the baby "Moses" because she drew him out of the water. She loved the baby boy. Moses was reared in Pharaoh's house as her son.

Then the Egyptians made the Israelites work harder. Later, the Israelites cried out to God for help. God sent Moses to lead the Israelites out of Egypt.

God, through Moses and Aaron his brother, did very powerful, frightening and destructive things to the Egyptians because Pharaoh refused to let them go.

At God's command, Moses told Aaron to strike the water with his rod and God changed the water in the Nile river into blood. God also caused the land to be covered with frogs and did many other things through Moses. Then, when Pharaoh would still not let the Israelite people go, God caused the part of the country where the Egyptians lived to turn into thick darkness—like black fog. They could not see anything but the Israelites still had light.

Pharaoh still would not let the Israelites go and he made them work even harder.

Finally, Moses told Pharaoh, "God is going to kill all the Egyptian firstborn—man and beast. You will never see my face ever again," and he left.

Then God told Moses to tell the Israelites to sacrifice a lamb and put the blood on the two side doorposts and the top of the doorway of their houses. They were not to go out of their house until morning. God would pass over their houses and not allow the destroyer to kill their firstborn in the houses marked with blood on the doorway.

God called this night the Passover. At midnight God killed all the firstborn Egyptian of men and animals. As the Egyptians cried loudly, Pharaoh told the Israelites they could leave. Remember, Pharaoh had Israelite babies and children killed. So as punishment, God judged the Egyptians for killing the Israelite children by killing their firstborn.

Out of Egypt and into the Wilderness

In the morning, the Israelites assembled in the city of Rameses. They left the next night when the Israelites were ready. They started their journey out of Egypt under a full moon with their cattle, sheep and the things they could take that the Egyptians gave them. They were very happy and sang praises to God who set them free after hundreds of years of hard work. God, led the Israelites by night with a pillar of fire and by day with a pillar of cloud.

The Israelites walked in the wilderness to a place where there was water blocking their way. The water was the Red Sea. The Egyptians then came after the Israelites. The Israelites were trapped and very frightened! Moses called out to the people, "Stand still and see the way God will save you." God moved the pillar of fire and the cloud between the Israelites and the Egyptians.

God told Moses to stretch out his hand above the water of the sea. God caused a strong east wind to blow all night. The water divided and the ground became dry. The Israelites walked across on dry ground between the walls of water.

The Egyptians chased after the Israelites to get them to come back as their slaves. The Egyptians went after the Israelites into the sea where it was divided.

God told Moses, "Stretch out your hand over the sea, that the waters may come again upon the Egyptians and upon their chariots and horsemen."

Moses stretched out his hand and the waters covered the chariots and horsemen. All the Egyptians who followed the Israelites were drowned.

God Spoke the Ten Commandments

Then God led the Israelites on through the wilderness. God told Moses to come to the mountain called Mount Sinai. From the top of the mountain, God spoke his Ten Commandments. Then He gave Moses two flat tables of stone that had the Ten Commandments written by the finger of God. The Ten Commandments tell everyone how to live so each one can love God and love each other.

THE TEN COMMANDMENTS

(Love to God)

1. You shall have no other gods before me to worship them.

2. Do not make any idols.

3. Do not take God's name in vain.

4. Remember the Sabbath day to keep it holy, remembering God, and that He has made everything. The Sabbath is a special time to learn God's way. Six days were made for work; the Seventh Day was made for rest.

5. Honor your father and mother.

(Love to People)

6. Do not murder any person.

7. Do not commit adultery.

8. Do not steal.

9. Do not tell lies and do not say wrong things about people.

10. Do not covet something that belongs to someone else.

God told the Israelites which animals are clean or good for food, such as cattle, sheep and goats. God told the people the ways to know which meat is good to eat. The animals must chew the cud and have cloven hooves. The fish that are good to eat must have fins and scales. That is how we know which meat is clean to eat.

"Do not eat blood or fat," God told the people.

God commanded the people to keep His Sabbath and Holy Days to learn about His great plan for all people.

God gave the Israelites lots of laws so they would know how to stop sickness from spreading and how to be clean.

Clean meat, which is good for people to eat, comes from these animals...

Unclean meat, which is <u>not good</u> for people to eat, comes from these animals...

... and many other animals.

...and many other animals.

53

Out of the Wilderness
and into the Promised Land

Because the Israelites sinned and Moses "struck" the rock for water they wandered in the wilderness for forty years. God fed them with bread from heaven called Manna. At last, God let them go into the Promised Land where they built houses and grew gardens, orchards and vineyards.

The Israelites obeyed God for a while, but then they started doing what they wanted and forgot God. They disobeyed His laws and way of life, so they had poverty and wars.

Manna tasted like wafers made with honey.

God appointed men to be priests and judges to guide and direct the Israelites under His direction. Sometimes the Israelites obeyed and all went well. Other times the Israelites would disobey God and trouble would come. When trouble came, the people would cry out to God for help.

Samuel as a Child

Sometimes God starts using a person when they are a very young child.

Hannah prayed to God very fervently for a child and God answered her prayers. She gave birth to a son. His name was Samuel. His mother dedicated him to God's service at the tabernacle when he was a child.

God talked to Samuel when he was only seven or eight years old. Samuel listened to what God told him. Samuel learned how to do the work in the tabernacle when he was growing up. He grew up to be a priest, judge and prophet for Israel.

Eli was the priest at the time that Samuel was young. After Samuel became a priest, God destroyed Eli and his sons for their wicked, evil deeds. They did not respect God and disobeyed Him.

God wanted Samuel to lead Israel in righteousness. He listened to God's instruction and told Israel how to please God.

Israel Wants a King

Later, the Israelites saw that the nations around them had kings to rule over them. The elders of Israel said to the prophet Samuel, "Give us a king like the other nations." God warned them saying, "You shall get a king, but a king that will take your children and make them work. And he will take your land, tents and houses, and you'll cry out to God for help and God will not hear you." The people still wanted a king.

The first king the Israelites had was Saul. He was a good king at first, but later he became a bad king because he didn't obey God.

King David

A boy named David was out in the field looking after his father's sheep when the prophet Samuel, who obeyed God, came to him. God had chosen David to be king over Israel.

During a war against the Philistines, David took some food to his brothers who were in the army. David found all the army of Israel standing back because they were afraid of a giant named Goliath. David, who had killed a lion and a bear with God's help, was bold and picked up five smooth stones and put them into his shepherd's bag. David put a stone in his sling and ran at the giant calling out, "The God of Israel will help me kill you, the enemy of the living God." The stone David hurled with his sling hit the giant Goliath in the forehead and he fell down dead.

When Goliath's army saw that Goliath was dead they turned and ran.

David wrote many songs and stories called Psalms, which tell us a lot about God and how that following His way is the way of right behavior.

God caused David to write, "The Law of the Lord is perfect, restoring the mind. The Word of the Lord is sure, making wise the simple."

David was a good king for a long time. Then he did some bad things, but he became very sorry and repented and followed God's way. Since then God has made sure that one of David's family has always been seated on the throne of David.

When David died, his son Solomon became king. God gave Solomon understanding to give wise answers and work out problems. God told Solomon how to build a house to the glory of God. The house was called a temple. The temple was very beautiful, with a lot of gold and many shining stones on it.

God blessed Solomon with lots of money, gold, and many other things because he asked God to make him wise to answer the people in the right way.

God caused Solomon to write many true wise words that show the best way to live, called Proverbs. Solomon wrote, "Where people cannot see what the future holds or the reasons why, they will perish; but he that keeps Gods law, happy is he."

Solomon also wrote, "He who does what is right cares about how his animals are treated, but the wicked man does not care and his ways are cruel."

The Holy Bible

Many more kings ruled Israel and Judah. Some obeyed God and everything went well. When a bad king would come to the throne and disobey God, then the people sinned and would have trouble, drought and war.

A bad king using witchcraft.

God raised up prophets to speak and write warnings of what was going to happen later and why. God said a child would be born Who would become the Savior of all mankind. He would grow up and teach us about God.

Daniel in the Lions' Den

Babylon was conquered by Darius. He was king, but did not understand about the true God. Daniel, a captive Israelite, was a good man and he obeyed God.

King Darius put Daniel as first president. The other two presidents and the princes were jealous and planned to get rid of Daniel. They wrote a royal statute and flattered the King so he signed it into law. No one was to ask anything of anyone or any god except of King Darius for 30 days or else they would be thrown into the lion's den.

Daniel still prayed to God every day and obeyed God. The evil presidents told the King that Daniel prayed to God three times a day. The King liked Daniel and did not want the lions to eat him, but he had to obey his own law. When the presidents threw Daniel into the lions' den, the King told Daniel that his God would deliver him.

Very early the next morning King Darius ran to the lions' den and called out, "Daniel, servant of the living God, is your God able to save you from the lions?" Then Daniel said, "My God has sent His angel, and has shut the lions' mouths..." Then the King was very happy and told the men to get Daniel out quickly. Next, the king ordered the evil presidents to be thrown to the hungry lions. The lions ate them and all their families.

Then King Darius wrote a decree stating that everyone in the kingdom should tremble and fear before the God of Daniel, for He is the living God, Who is steadfast forever.

Daniel prayed to God while the lions slept

God told the prophets to write about the King of truth and righteousness Who would come to be the great Teacher.

God told the prophets to warn Israel of the trouble they would bring upon themselves if they did not obey Him. But Israel again began to seek the heathen gods and pagan ideas of the countries near them. Again the Israelites forgot the true way of God.

Long ago God caused the prophet Samuel to write, "Obeying God is better than sacrifice, and to listen to Him than the fat of rams." Doing what God says is far better than following our own ideas. Rebelling against God is like the evil of witchcraft and being stubborn is like the evil of worshipping idols.

Because the Israelites went against God, He said, "I will return to my place until the people admit their guilt and seek my face."

"Therefore will I also deal in fury. My eye shall not spare, neither will I have pity, and though they cry in my ears with a loud voice, yet I will not hear them because of the evil of their ways in forgetting Me and My laws."

Remember back at the beginning when Adam and Eve disobeyed God in the Garden of Eden? They ate fruit from the Tree of the Knowledge of Good and Evil. God the Son had to triumph over the evil things, called sin, which Adam and Eve had done.

3,500 years later, God the Son would be born as a baby and grow up to be a man and then die to pay for all the terrible sins and trouble, killing, war, sickness, fighting, and death that continues with all people even today.

Trouble comes from disobeying God and following Satan. God the Son was going to give all His people the chance to repent and return to follow God.

God has made all things. God knows far more than any person and knows what is best for everyone.

Satan is very sneaky and evil. He tries to tempt everyone to follow things that sound religious or good but which are really disobedience to God and not the way God told us to worship Him.

God the Father and God the Son love and care for all people. They want all people to stop following Satan and learn that God's way is the only way to bring lasting happiness.

God says, "Turn you, turn you from your evil ways, for why will you die?" (Ezekiel 33:11)

Trouble comes from disobeying God.

"And God sent the man out from the garden to work the ground."

"Cursed is the ground; thorns and thistles shall it bring forth."

"And God saw that the wickedness of man was very evil. The imagination of the thoughts of his heart was only evil continually."

Birth of Jesus

In a city called Nazareth there was a woman named Mary. God sent His angel, Gabriel, to tell Mary she would have a baby boy. Gabriel told Mary that God's Power and Spirit would cause her to have a baby.

Mary was going to marry a man named Joseph. Later Joseph married Mary and they went to a town named Bethlehem to try to find a place to camp for the Feast of God. The only place they could find was in a stable.

Mary gave birth to the baby boy, wrapped him in cloth and put him in a manger. The angel of the Lord had told Joseph and Mary to call His name Jesus, which means, "the One Who saves." He was also called Christ, which means, "the Anointed One."

Life of Jesus

From the time Jesus was a baby, He was taught in vision directly by God the Father early every morning. He was never instructed by a man or rabbi. Mary, His mother, did teach Jesus some things as a small child.

Jesus grew to be a very wise and sensible man. He became the greatest teacher because He had come from God the Father and understood more than any man. Jesus told the people about God and how He wants everyone to live. Jesus was given great power by God the Father to heal sick people so they could get well and heal blind people so they could see and heal deaf people so they could hear. Jesus showed that following what He said is the most important step to knowing the true way of God. We are to love Jesus and God the Father with all our hearts.

Jesus Christ will give the gift of life forever to all people who love God and obey His laws and way of life.

Jesus said that the time is coming when God will get rid of Satan and his demons and teach all people God's way. Jesus came to tell us to repent and obey God. He came to tell us about the time when He, Jesus, will change this evil world. He came to die on the cross to pay for all the sins and disobedience to God so that people can know the true God.

"I can see!" "I can talk!"

Death of Jesus

A lot of people did not want to hear Jesus, and others did not want to believe Him. Satan stirred up the people and they killed Jesus by beating Him, whipping Him and nailing Him to a big timber post made into a cross. Finally, a soldier thrust a spear under His rib to make certain He was dead.

At that time a great darkness came over the earth. When Jesus died, a thick curtain in the Temple was ripped from top to bottom. The earth shook and rocks split open. A very frightened soldier said, "Truly, this was the Son of God."

Joseph of Arimathaea came and took Jesus' body down from the post, put ointment on it and wrapped it in cloth. He then put Jesus' body in a tomb and rolled a round stone in the doorway.

Resurrection of Jesus

Three days and three nights went by, and then God the Father brought Jesus back to life.

Jesus told His disciples that He would go back to heaven and be with God the Father again. Jesus said He would come back to Earth in the last days and set up His kingdom. Satan and his demons would be removed and put in the prison of the great abyss.

Jesus told His disciples that people who obey God's way will be given life forever and be leaders when He comes back to earth. Jesus finished talking to them and as they looked, He was taken up into heaven in a cloud and out of their sight.

While His disciples kept looking up, two angels in white clothing stood nearby. The two angels said, "Jesus will come back just as you have seen Him go."

By the time Jesus comes back there will be much learning, discovery and the making of many clever machines and devices. The world will be full of Satan's evil ideas and most people will follow them, thinking they are doing well. Many people will become rich because God promised Abraham that He would give good land and many other blessings to Abraham's children.

Satan does not want people to learn the true way of God. It is the true way of God that leads to eternal life by God the Father and Jesus Christ.

Until the set time for Jesus to return, Satan will continue to influence the people to do evil. Satan loves to get people to put God's name on their evil religions and think they are doing what God wants them to do.

There will be wars, droughts, floods, and famine. There will also be much sickness, pain and death because the people are following Satan's evil way and not God's way.

God has allowed Satan to blind the eyes of most of the people for now, but when Satan is put away God will open the eyes of the people and teach them His way.

Most people do not want to believe that Jesus is coming back.

"In the last days there will come mockers doing whatever they like, asking, 'Where is the promise of His coming?'" Everything is the same since the beginning of mankind.

There will be a very evil man who will call himself the "Christ", a false messiah or savior, and will deceive the whole world.

Before Jesus comes back, he will send two men with great power, and they will prophesy for about three and a half years.

Then there will be great troubles, more than ever before, and unless God stops the terrible destruction, no one will be left alive. Then, as the sun shines from the east to the west, so will it be when Jesus comes back to earth. And then everyone will fight Him.

Also, the sun will be darkened, the moon will not give light and the stars will fall from heaven.

Then Jesus will come back on the clouds of heaven with great power and great glory. Jesus said He would send His angels with the loud sound of a trumpet to gather, from everywhere around the world, the people God has chosen because they obeyed Him.

God will raise from the dead everyone who obeyed Him. Noah, Abraham, Isaac, Jacob, David and all the apostles and true believers are the many people God will bring back to life when Jesus returns.

Then God will send His wrath on the disobedient people of the world. "Behold the day of the Lord comes both with wrath and fierce anger to lay the land bare and destroy the disobedient out of it."

But God will protect all people and children who love and obey Him.

Our Father in Heaven, we come before you in prayer...

To tell us of Jesus' return He caused the apostle John to write, "I saw heaven opened and behold a white horse, and (Jesus Christ) Who sat upon the horse was called Faithful and True... (Jesus') eyes were as a flame of fire and on His head were many crowns. And (Jesus') name is the Word of God."

Greatly blessed and spiritually pure (the ones who are thinking the way God wants us to think) are the ones who have part in the first resurrection...they shall be priests of God and of Christ, and shall reign with Him a thousand years to bring peace and happiness to all people.

At the end many people will see that God's way is right and they will change their ways to obey Him.

Satan Locked Up

Satan the devil will be caught by God's angel and bound with a huge chain. Satan will be thrown into what is called a bottomless pit. He will not be able to cause people to sin any more. The evil angels, called demons, that help Satan now, will be thrown into the bottomless pit with him. A seal will be put on Satan and his demons so they will be locked up for a thousand years.

The world will then be without Satan and his demons. Then there will be love and peace.

Jesus Christ Rules the World

Jesus Christ will be King and rule over the whole world. There will be no more wars. He will have all power so He can heal the nations. Anyone that has anything wrong with them will be healed. They will be completely well.

God says, "Be strong, fear not. God will come with a reward... the eyes of the blind shall be able to see, the ears of the deaf will hear, the lame man shall leap like a deer, the tongues of the people who cannot talk will be able to speak. In the wilderness water will break out, and streams will flow in the desert. The dry ground shall become a pool and the thirsty land (will have) springs of water with grass, and reeds, and rushes."

"The wolf also shall live with the lamb and the leopard shall lie down with the kid. The sucking child shall play on the hole of the asp. The weaned child shall put his hand in the vipers den and will not be hurt. The cow and bear shall feed and their young ones shall lie down together. The lion shall eat grass like the bullock. They shall not hurt nor destroy anything when Jesus Christ is King over the earth."

The understanding of God's way on how to live will be all over the earth like the water covers the sea. The nature of animals will be changed. The land will become fertile, there will be plenty of good food for everyone and there will be rain in due season.

Great White Throne Judgment

After 1,000 years, God will bring back to life all the rest of the people who have ever lived. They will be shown God's way and they will have to choose whether to obey God or not. Then there will be no more fears or sadness and no more suffering ever again.

Eye has not seen, ear has not heard, neither has it entered into the mind of people the things God has prepared for those who are really doing what He has told us. No one will disobey God anymore. There will be everlasting righteousness.

God will live with people at last.

The body that dies and decays will be replaced by one that will <u>not</u> die and <u>cannot</u> decay. So will come to pass the saying, "Death is swallowed up in victory."

God will wipe away all tears.

In the judgment, every person will be accountable for every idle word they have spoken.

A man named John saw a great white throne in a vision. He saw the dead, small and great, standing before God: and the books were open... and the sea gave up the dead and all that were in it; and death and the grave delivered up the dead which were in them: and they were judged every man according to his works.

The way of life forever is to stay away from evil and replace doing evil with doing well.

God wants all people to learn to obey His commandments, trust Him, and fear to disobey.

Be humble and patient. Be sad for the trouble caused by people and Satan.

Be of a gentle, mild, peace-making attitude. Be eagerly wanting God's way. Be merciful, forgiving, kind, generous, helpful, pure in heart, longsuffering and slow to anger.

God wants us to seek first His kingdom and His righteousness.

God wants all people to resist the downward pull of disobeying Him.

Eternal life is a gift from God that He gives to those who love and obey Him.

Fruits of the Spirit

God's Pathway
or
the Way
of
the World—

Which Will You
Choose?

God's Pathway

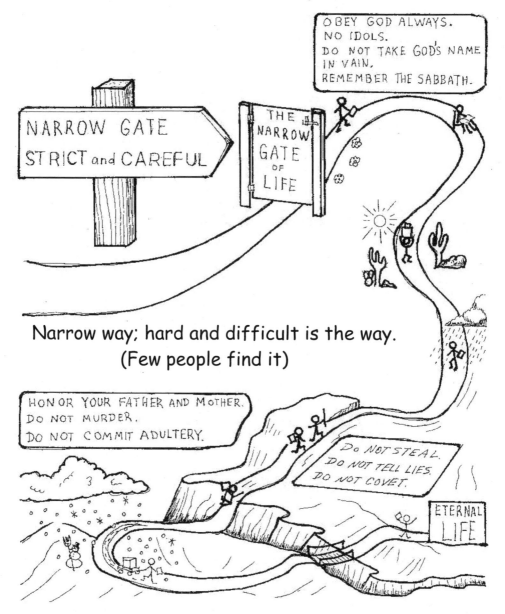

Narrow way; hard and difficult is the way.
(Few people find it)

God says, "I set before you this day, life and good, and death and evil. In that God commands you this day to obey the Lord your God; to walk in His ways, and to know His commands and His statutes, and His judgments that you may live."

The World's Way

Today, in this world, Satan is trying to get people to go the wrong way, which brings death forever. Satan is trying to trick people to be disobedient to God, to be selfish, impatient, double-minded, stubborn, boastful, sneaky, accusing, violent, greedy, mean, angry without proper reason, trouble-making, bullying, bossy, unkind, cruel, overpowering, hateful, rebellious, vain, deceitful, following idols, using witchcraft and practicing false religions. Satan wants us to love the evil way, the pride and the vanity of this world.

Broad way: They don't care. They do what they like. They follow the way of the world. (Many people follow this easy way.)

Analyzing Peoples' False Ideas About God

One reason God gave people the commandments is so we will turn from our disobedience to Him. Learn to obey God's commands and understand that Jesus Christ's death and resurrection has paid the penalty for the evil things that Adam and Eve and the rest of us have done by disobeying God.

Jesus Christ has given all of us the chance to turn away from sin and obey God and be in His family—the family of God.

"Behold, the Lord's hand is not shortened that it cannot save. Nor His ear heavy that it cannot hear, but our wrong-doing has separated us from our God." Our disobedience causes God to hide His face from us that He may not hear us.

Some people say that when a person dies he or she goes to heaven. But God says, "The dead know nothing." No man has gone up to heaven except God the Son, who is Jesus Christ, who came down from heaven.

Some people say Jesus was born on Christmas day, but He wasn't. Christmas day is a party day from a heathen idea which started long before Jesus was born. God says, "Do not learn the ways of the heathen." The heathen are people who do not believe God. Scriptures show that Jesus was born about the Feast of Trumpets—a Holy Day of God

Some people say Jesus rose from the dead on Easter. Actually, Easter is a party time for an evil woman-god called the queen of heaven. God the Father and Jesus Christ hate these parties because they come from very bad ideas that can lead people away from God. To know right from wrong God says, "Prove all things, and hold fast that which is good." Jesus was resurrected at the end of the Sabbath Day, three nights and three days after He was put into the grave.

Some people say Sunday is the day God told us to keep as a rest from work and to learn His way. Sunday is the day people use to worship the sun. God says, "Do not follow the ideas of other people or your own ideas." God says, "Trust in God with all your heart and strength." God says to worship Him and rest on His Sabbath day.

Some people say the world started with a big bang but God created the world and all things. Long ago God spoke to a man named Job. Job thought he knew a lot of things. God asked Job, "Where were you when I laid the foundations of the earth? Have you entered into the springs of the sea? Have you given the horse his strength? Have you clothed his neck with thunder?"

Job answered God, "I know that you can do everything and that no thought can be kept from you."

Before we believe what people tell us, we need to prove the truth with the Bible.

Some people trust in crossed fingers and touching or knocking on wood for good luck. God says, "Go not after other gods to serve them and to worship them. Don't make God angry with your works and God will not punish you."

Some people think that by themselves they have the strength and ability to do the things they need to do. Everything we have has been given to us. All matter has been made by God. God says, "For the world is mine and all that's in it is mine." All things were created by God and for His pleasure.

Some people say their religion is from God, but it is not. Satan is very cunning and he fools people to think that his ideas are from the true God, but they are not. God says to test those ideas to see if they are of God.

Some people seek revenge. God says, "Vengeance is mine. I will repay."

These are some FALSE religious practices!

Many people follow the teachings of men. They take the name of God and some of the words of the Bible to make their religion sound like it comes from God. But God says, "Because these people do not love the truth and do not know that God can save them, God will send strong error." Therefore, they will believe lies. God will allow these people to believe wrong things because they do not want to believe Him. God says to the person who obeys Him, "I will allow you to eat of the Tree of Life."

To people who are overcoming wrong ideas, human nature, and Satan's temptations and keep God's way to the end, God will give them power over the nations.

Even though this is the end of this little book, learning God's way takes all our life. When Jesus Christ returns and is King, He shall reign over His entire kingdom FOREVER.

And there shall be **NO END!**
My Personal Bible Pathway

God's Special Commandment for Children

Children,

Obey your parents in the Lord,

For this is right.

Honor your Father and your Mother,

Which is the

First Commandment with a Promise,

That it may be well with you,

And that you may live long

on the earth.

 Ephesians 6:1-3

My Personal Bible Pathway

I know that there is a great all powerful God Who created the heavens and the earth. He created the land, the seas, the air and all that is in them.

I know that God gave us His laws and commandments so I would know how to do good.

I know that God loves me and all little children. He expects me to be obedient and it is really important for me to obey my parents. When you think about it, God is my Heavenly Father and that means I should obey Him always. The best way I can show my love to Him is by being obedient and God blesses me when I am obedient.

I know I should live by the "Golden Rule" and the golden rule is for me to treat others like I want to be treated. I know I should treat other people good and not lie or take anything that is not mine.

I know the Bible tells me that God will answer when I pray. I also know that I should pray every day for God's help. God also wants me to pray for health or needs of other people. It doesn't have to be a fancy prayer, but one that I really mean from my heart.

I know that to learn what I should do, I must read and study the Holy Bible. Every day I need to read at least a few verses. I know I should first pray that God will help me to understand what I read.

I know that God can hear my prayers no matter where I am or even what time of day or night it is. I know that I should pray that God will help me solve any problem I might have. He may not answer like I want, but He will take care of me the best way.

I know that whatever I do, I should try to do it to the best of my ability and really try hard. God will help me when I am trying to do my best.

I know I am to do all these things and I pray that God will help me to do them. I know that when I fail, I can go talk to God about it and when I am really sorry and promise to try to do better, God will help me.

Now I will pray that God will help me to know what I should do and help me to do it. Please be reading me the Bible so God can teach me.

I must be strong and stand firm when my friends or classmates tease and make fun of me. Because I don't act like they do.

I know that "Jesus Loves Me!" I love Him and always want to obey Him.

How to Pray

Jesus gave us the following example of how to pray in Matthew 5:9-13. Therefore, you are to pray after this manner:

"Our Father Who is in heaven, hallowed be Your name;

Your kingdom come; Your will be done on earth, as it is in heaven;

Give us this day our daily bread;

And forgive us our debts, as we also forgive our debtors;

And lead us not into temptation, but rescue us from the evil one. For Yours is the kingdom and the power and the glory forever. Amen."

This is an example of how to pray, but we don't need to just repeat these exact words. We

 need to praise God and ask for forgiveness of our sins. Then tell Him what we need and thank Him for all He is doing for us.

Special Way to Study the Book of Proverbs

The "Book of Proverbs" contains many very good teachings about the "Way of God." Many of the teachings are presented in a way to teach me right from wrong; good from evil. These teachings deal with everyday life situations and are very beneficial for all, especially children and teens.

The simple way to study is to read the "Chapter" matching the "Day" of the month. That is, on day one of a month, read chapter one. On day two, read chapter two and throughout the days of a month. If you miss the study on a day, just skip to the chapter matching the current day of the month.

Not all months have 31 days, so you may read chapter 31 in addition to chapter 30 on day 30 or else skip chapter 31 until the next month.

This study plan provides a regular reading and study schedule. God will bless your efforts.

The Ten Commandments
Exodus 20:1-17

And God spoke all these words, saying,

1. I *am* the LORD your God, Who brought you out of the land of Egypt, out of the house of bondage. You shall have no other gods before Me.
2. You shall not make for yourselves any graven image, or any likeness of *anything* that *is* in the heavens above, or that *is* in the earth beneath, or that *is* in the waters under the earth. You shall not bow yourself down to them, nor serve them, for I, the LORD your God *am* a jealous God, visiting the iniquity of the fathers upon the children unto the third and fourth generation of those who hate Me, but showing mercy to thousands of those who love Me and keep My commandments.
3. You shall not take the name of the LORD your God in vain, for the LORD will not hold him guiltless who takes His name in vain.
4. Remember the Sabbath day to keep it holy. Six days you shall labor and do all your work. But the seventh day *is* the Sabbath of the LORD your God. In it you shall not do any work, you, nor your son, nor your daughter; your manservant, nor your maidservant, nor your livestock, nor the stranger within your gates; for *in* six days the LORD made the heaven and the earth, the sea, and all that *is* in them, and rested the seventh day. Therefore the LORD blessed the Sabbath day and sanctified it.
5. Honor your father and your mother so that your days may be long upon the land which the LORD your God gives you.
6. You shall not murder.
7. You shall not commit adultery.
8. You shall not steal.
9. You shall not bear false witness against your neighbor.
10. You shall not covet your neighbor's house. You shall not covet your neighbor's wife, nor his manservant, nor his maidservant, nor his ox, nor his donkey, nor anything that *is* your neighbor's.

<u>What Should I Pray About
And Who Should I Pray To?</u>

I need to pray to God the Father
and Jesus Christ every day:

I pray for:
- Protection for my family and me,
- That God will help me to do what is right,
- That God will bless my family and me,
- That God will help us be healthy,
- That God will make those who are sick better,
- That God will bring his wonderful kingdom soon,
- That God will bless me with wisdom,
- That God will bless me with His love,
- That God will look after me in the future and keep me safe,
- That God will forgive me when I do something wrong,
- That God will provide a good husband/wife for me when I grow up.

I remember to thank God for all the things He provides for me:
- A home to live in,
- Healthy food to eat,
- Safety and peace,
- Clothes to wear,
- My mom and dad,
- My brothers and sisters,
- Knowledge of the truth,
- My Bible that helps me learn God's way.

I remember to praise and honor God for He made me and loves me.